CONTENTS

GROUP DIRECTORY

Write your name on this page. Pass your books around and ask your group members to fill in their names and contact information in each other's books.

Your Name: _____

Name: _____   Name: _____
Address: _____   Address: _____
City: _____   City: _____
Zip Code: _____   Zip Code: _____
Home Phone: _____   Home Phone: _____
Mobile Phone: _____   Mobile Phone: _____
E-Mail: _____   E-Mail: _____

Name: _____   Name: _____
Address: _____   Address: _____
City: _____   City: _____
Zip Code: _____   Zip Code: _____
Home Phone: _____   Home Phone: _____
Mobile Phone: _____   Mobile Phone: _____
E-Mail: _____   E-Mail: _____

Name: _____   Name: _____
Address: _____   Address: _____
City: _____   City: _____
Zip Code: _____   Zip Code: _____
Home Phone: _____   Home Phone: _____
Mobile Phone: _____   Mobile Phone: _____
E-Mail: _____   E-Mail: _____

Name: _____   Name: _____
Address: _____   Address: _____
City: _____   City: _____
Zip Code: _____   Zip Code: _____
Home Phone: _____   Home Phone: _____
Mobile Phone: _____   Mobile Phone: _____
E-Mail: _____   E-Mail: _____

Name: _____   Name: _____
Address: _____   Address: _____
City: _____   City: _____
Zip Code: _____   Zip Code: _____
Home Phone: _____   Home Phone: _____
Mobile Phone: _____   Mobile Phone: _____
E-Mail: _____   E-Mail: _____

Name: _____   Name: _____
Address: _____   Address: _____
City: _____   City: _____
Zip Code: _____   Zip Code: _____
Home Phone: _____   Home Phone: _____
Mobile Phone: _____   Mobile Phone: _____
E-Mail: _____   E-Mail: _____

You Have Opened the Door to Great Beginnings!

I am thrilled that you have chosen this resource. It will catapult your group toward Christian Community. You may wonder about the genesis of this Great Beginnings concept. While serving Living Hope Baptist Church in Bowling Green, Kentucky, I sat with our first generation of small-group leaders. During our conversation a key question continued to arise: "How could we arrive at Christian Community more quickly?" Each of the groups had created various unique, fun, and meaningful experiences. As this great team of leaders merged their ideas, we realized the need for a resource that would reveal what small groups were and launch groups from the beginning toward authentic community. It would include:

- A covenant to unleash the power of commitment
- A resources profile to uncover the uniqueness of each individual God brought into the group
- A spiritual gifts assessment to increase effectiveness of service within the group
- A mapping of our personal stories to help us deepen our relationships and engage our God-given passions
- A discussion of our needs to jump-start the process of sharing real life together
- An understanding of life in Christian Community

Incorporating all of these elements into one six-week study seemed like genius. We all knew that having these vital experiences in the first six weeks of a group's life would establish what group life should be like and compel it to happen more quickly.

Today that study has become a reality. What you have in hand is a resource that will allow the people in your group to know one another's stories, resources, giftedness, passions, and needs in the first six weeks of doing life together.

In the leader notes at the back of the book, you'll find some general leader helps as well as tips for each session. These will help you enhance the group experience in each meeting.

Be aware that the dialogue in each week's study was written as though I was leading each group session. In essence, it's written from the small-group leader's perspective. Reading this material aloud in the meeting may be helpful, especially for first-time group leaders.

I hope this study does all we dreamed it would do for you and your group!

Rick

Rick Howerton
Director of Events and Training, Serendipity House

5

Welcome to Community

Meeting together with a group of people to study God's Word and experience life together is an exciting adventure.

A small group is ... *a group of people unwilling to settle for anything less than redemptive community*.

Core Values

Community:
God is relational, so He created us to live in relationship with Him and each other. Authentic community involves *sharing life together* and *connecting* on many levels with the people in our group.

Group Process:
Developing authentic community requires a step-by-step process. It's a journey of sharing our stories with each other and learning together.

Stages of Development:
Every healthy group goes through various stages as it matures over a period of months or years. We begin with the *birth* of a new group, deepen our relationships in the *growth* and *development* stages, and ultimately *multiply* to form other new groups.

Interactive Bible Study:
God provided the Bible as an instruction manual of life. We need to deepen our understanding of God's Word. People learn and remember more as they wrestle with truth and learn from others. The process of Bible discovery and group interaction will enhance our growth.

Experiential Growth:

The goal of studying the Bible together is not merely a quest for knowledge, but should result in real life change. Beyond merely reading, studying, and dissecting the Bible, being a disciple of Christ involves reunifying knowledge with experience. We do this by bringing our questions to God, opening a dialogue with our hearts (instead of killing our desires), and utilizing other ways to listen to God speak to us (group interaction, nature, art, movies, circumstances, etc.). Experiential growth is always grounded in the Bible as God's primary means of revelation and our ultimate truth-source.

The Power of God:

Our processes and strategies will be ineffective unless we invite and embrace the presence and power of God. In order to experience community and growth, Jesus needs to be the centerpiece of our group experiences and the Holy Spirit must be at work.

Redemptive Community:

Healing best happens within the context of community and in relationship. Key aspects of our spiritual development include seeing ourselves through the eyes of others, sharing our stories, and ultimately being set free from the secrets and the lies we embrace that enslave our souls.

Mission:

God has invited us into a larger story with a great mission. It is a mission that involves setting captives free and healing the broken-hearted (Isaiah 61:1-2). However, we can only join in this mission to the degree that we've let Jesus bind up our wounds and set us free. As a group experiences true redemptive community, other people will be attracted to that group, and through that group to Jesus. We should be alert to inviting others while we maintain (and continue to fill) an "empty chair" in our meetings to remind us of others who need to encounter God and authentic Christian Community.

SHARING YOUR STORIES

The sessions in *Great Beginnings* are designed to help you share a little of your personal lives with the other people in your group each time you meet. Through your time together, each member of the group is encouraged to move from low risk, less personal sharing to higher risk communication. Real community will not develop apart from increasing intimacy within the group over time.

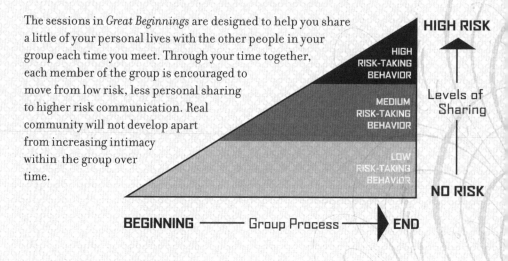

SHARING YOUR LIVES

As you share your lives together during this time, it is important to recognize that it is God who has brought each person to this group, gifting the individuals to play a vital role in the group (1 Corinthians 12:1). Each of you was uniquely designed to contribute in your own unique way to building into the lives of the other people in your group. As you get to know one another better, consider the following four areas that will be unique for each person. These areas will help you get a "grip" how you can better support others and how they can support you.

G – Spiritual Gifts: God has given you unique spiritual gifts (1 Corinthians 12; Romans 12:3-8; Ephesians 4:1-16; etc.)

R – Resources: You have resources that perhaps only you can share, including skills, abilities, possessions, money, and time (Acts 2:44-47; Ecclesiastes 4:9-12, etc.)

I – Individual Experiences: You have past experiences, both good and bad, that God can use to strengthen others (2 Corinthians 1:3-7; Romans 8:28, etc.)

P – Passions: There are things that excite and motivate you. God has given you those desires and passions to use for His purposes (Psalm 37:4,23; Proverbs 3:5-6,13-18; etc.)

Your Group's G-R-I-P Profile

G – **Spiritual Gifts**
R – **Resources** (skills, abilities, possessions, money, and time)
I – **Individual Experiences**
P – **Passions**

Name: _____
G: _____
R: _____
I: _____
P: _____

Name: _____
G: _____
R: _____
I: _____
P: _____

Name: _____
G: _____
R: _____
I: _____
P: _____

Name: _____
G: _____
R: _____
I: _____
P: _____

Name: _____
G: _____
R: _____
I: _____
P: _____

Name: _____
G: _____
R: _____
I: _____
P: _____

Name: _____
G: _____
R: _____
I: _____
P: _____

Name: _____
G: _____
R: _____
I: _____
P: _____

Name: _____
G: _____
R: _____
I: _____
P: _____

Name: _____
G: _____
R: _____
I: _____
P: _____

Name: _____
G: _____
R: _____
I: _____
P: _____

Name: _____
G: _____
R: _____
I: _____
P: _____

STAGES OF GROUP LIFE

Each healthy small group will move through various stages as it matures. There is no prescribed time frame for moving through these stages because each group is unique.

Birth Stage:
This is the time in which group members form relationships and begin to develop community.

Multiply Stage:
The group begins the multiplication process. Members pray about their involvement in establishing new groups. The new groups begin the cycle again with the Birth Stage.

Growth Stage:
Here the group members begin to care for one another as they learn what it means to apply what they have discovered through Bible study, shared experiences, worship, and prayer

Develop Stage:
The Bible study and shared experiences deepen while the group members develop their gifts and skills. The group explores ways to invite neighbors, friends, and coworkers to meetings.

Subgrouping: If you have more than 12 people at a meeting, Serendipity House recommends dividing into smaller subgroups after the "Breaking the Ice" segment. Ask one person to be the leader of each subgroup, following the "Leader" directions for the session. The Group Leader should bring the subgroups back together for the closing. Subgrouping is also very useful when more openness and intimacy is required. The "Connecting" segment in each session is a great time to divide into smaller groups of 4 to 6 people.

Group Meeting

Each of your group meetings will include a four-part agenda.

1. Breaking the Ice:
This section includes fun, uplifting questions to warm up the group and help group members get to know one another better as they begin the journey of becoming a connected community. These questions prepare the group for meaningful discussion throughout the session.

2. Discovering the Truth:
The heart of each session is the interactive Bible study time. The goal is for the group to discover biblical truths through open, discovery questions that lead to further investigation. The emphasis in this section is on understanding what the Bible says through interaction within your group.

To help the group experience a greater sense of community, it is important for everybody to participate in the "Discovering the Truth" and "Embracing the Truth" discussions. Even though people in a group have differing levels of biblical knowledge, it is vital that group members encourage each other share what they are observing, thinking, and feeling about the Bible passages. Scripture notes are provided at the end of each session to provide additional Bible understanding.

3. Embracing the Truth:
All study should direct group members to action and life change. This section continues the Bible study time, but with an emphasis on leading group members toward integrating the truths they have discovered into their lives. The questions are very practical and application-focused.

4. Connecting:
One of the key goals of this study to lead group members to grow closer to one another as the group develops a sense of community. This section focuses on further application, as well as opportunities for encouraging, supporting, and praying for one another.

BONUS – Taking it Home:
Between several sessions, there is some homework for group members. This typically includes completing a brief individual assessment. These experiences are designed to reinforce the content of the session and help strengthen your group.

Meeting Planner

The leader or facilitator of our group is _____.
The apprentice facilitator for this group is _____.

We will meet on the following dates and times:

	Date	Day	Time
Session 1	_____	_____	_____
Session 2	_____	_____	_____
Session 3	_____	_____	_____
Session 4	_____	_____	_____
Session 5	_____	_____	_____
Session 6	_____	_____	_____

We will meet at:

Session 1	_____
Session 2	_____
Session 3	_____
Session 4	_____
Session 5	_____
Session 6	_____

Childcare will be arranged by:

Session 1	_____
Session 2	_____
Session 3	_____
Session 4	_____
Session 5	_____
Session 6	_____

Refreshments will be arranged by:

Session 1	_____
Session 2	_____
Session 3	_____
Session 4	_____
Session 5	_____
Session 6	_____

Bon Voyage!
Opening the Door to a New Adventure

We're about to undertake a life-changing voyage. Each of us has chosen to ascend the ladder that leads to the deck of the cruise ship Small Group, a floating party boat owned by the charter company Authentic Christianity. Once we leave the dock, there is no turning back. And once on board, jumping ship is out of the question because this adventure just wouldn't be the same without you.

Before we set sail, you deserve to know the expectations and responsibilities of each person on board. So, later in our session, we're going to unveil a covenant agreement—a pact that will make this expedition extraordinary. We'll also discover what a small group is. Most importantly, we'll set our eyes on our destination, Christian Community. Our map to this amazing island will be revealed a bit more each week as we travel together on this exciting journey of life.

Before we launch, let's find out a bit more about our fellow travelers. Each week we'll begin our study with a "Breaking the Ice" experience that will help us know each other better. All you have to do is play along. Would each of you answer a couple of questions? We'll discuss these one at a time so that everyone can share.

 ## BREAKING THE ICE   15 Minutes

LEADER: Be sure to read the introductory materials in the front of this book before the next session. To help your group members get to know one another better, have each one introduce him or herself and then take turns answering all of the "Breaking the Ice" questions. Be sure you don't skip the last one.

1. Which excursion appeals the most to you and why?
   _____ Hiking in the Rocky Mountains
   _____ Snorkeling at the Great Barrier Reef
   _____ Meandering through the Metropolitan Museum of Art
   _____ Shopping in New York City
   _____ Salmon fishing on the Kenai River in Alaska
   _____ Other (explain): _____

2. Which Starbucks® purchase would your best friend say most accurately describes you?

___ Café Americano – I tackle the hard stuff in life.

___ Toffee Nut Crème – There's a crazy side of me just waiting to erupt.

___ Coffee of the Day – I like being stylish.

___ Apple Juice – I may seem bland to you, but I enjoy helping everyone else remain healthy.

___ Pumpkin Spice Latte and a Blueberry Muffin - I thrive on diversity and am a multi-tasker.

___ Iced White Chocolate Mocha – I have led a complex life that hinders my ability to warm up quickly to other people.

___ Tazo® Chai Crème Frappuccino® Blended Tea – I like being different.

___ Other: _____

3. What promise did you make in your teen years that was the most difficult to keep? Why was it so difficult?

 # DISCOVERING THE TRUTH   **15-20 Minutes**

Our definition of a small group is, "A group of people unwilling to settle for anything less than redemptive community." Redemptive community is authentic and life-changing Christian Community. Many Christ-followers have been duped into believing they've experienced a redemptive Christian Community in their Bible study, Sunday School class, or church. The truth is they've experienced a community that is made up of Christians, but just being present in a group of Christians is not the depth of community we're aiming for.

I know I've experienced redemptive Christian Community when I'm as passionate about praying for you as I am about praying for myself, when I celebrate the extraordinary wins in your life as passionately as I celebrate my own victories, and when I find your tearstains on my shirt and mine on yours. In this sort of environment, your laughter rings in my ears and mine rings in yours. It is only when we pray for one another, hold each other accountable, respect one another, and look forward to our small-group meeting (so we can grow together and become more like Jesus) that we can say we've truly experienced the thrill of Christian Community.

Community According to ... Solomon?

Apart from Jesus, Solomon became the wisest man ever to live on this planet. In the Book of Ecclesiastes, he paints a profound image of what Christian Community looks like. Let's do a little evaluation of his depiction and find out what we can do in community that we cannot do alone. Check it out ...

LEADER: Select three people from your group to read Ecclesiastes 4:9-10. Ask for three volunteers to be reader 1, reader 2, and reader 3. Have them read the passage emphasizing the words "one," "two," and "three" when those words are spoken.

Readers 1 and 2:
⁹Two are better than one
   because they have a good reward for their efforts.

Reader 3:
¹⁰ For if either falls,
   his companion can lift him up;

Readers 1 and 2:
   but pity the one who falls
   without another to lift him up.
¹¹ Also, if two lie down together, they can keep warm;

Reader 3:
   but how can one person alone keep warm?
¹² And if somebody overpowers one person,

Readers 1 and 2:
   two can resist him.

Readers 1, 2, and 3:
A cord of three strands is not easily broken.

ECCLESIASTES 4:9-12

1. According to Ecclesiastes 4:10-12, what three situations might we might find ourselves in when we are living life alone?

2. In each of these situations, how would it be helpful to have a real friend there with you? What are the benefits of two people working together rather than one working alone?

3. Looking at the end of verse 12, we see that three people are even better than two to help us up when we've fallen ethically, spiritually, or physically. In your experience, why is this true? How can you create a life with a "cord of three strands"?

4. Why would you pity the people who find themselves alone in any of these situations?

EMBRACING THE TRUTH   15-20 Minutes

1. Was there a time in your life when you needed someone to pick you up, keep you warm, or help defend you? Share this experience with the group. Who helped you? What did they do for you? Describe your relationship with that person today.

2. Of the battles noted below, which ones might this group need to help you fight over the duration of our life together? Please explain.

____ Civil War - Sometimes I want secede from the union I have with an acquaintance.

____ Battle of the Sexes - Men really are from Mars, and women really are from Venus.

____ 9 to 5 War - I would love to go AWOL from my job right now.

____ Revolutionary War - My kids are trying to run my life.

____ Three-Day War - There's too much to do and too little time to do it in.

____ The Crusades - My religion is getting in the way of my Christianity.

____ Other: _____

3. What are some ways that we could strengthen and lift each other up in both good times and bad?

4. What could we do in a practical way to help you this week?

 # CONNECTING

15 minutes

> *LEADER: If people in the group are hesitant about agreeing to the covenant, give them the week to continue to read through the covenant, and then discuss it shortly at the next meeting. Be sure all group members agree to the covenant in the first three weeks of group meetings.*

The truth is, none of us were destined to stand alone. Even Jesus surrounded Himself with a few close friends, people He depended on to be by His side. We all require Christian Community. In order for our group to encounter this incredible lifestyle, we're going to need to reach an agreement on a few important principles and practices.

Covenanting together is vital to our experiencing Christian Community. When everyone embraces the goal of being in Christian Community, and everyone reads the same map to discover how to arrive there, we've traveled the first mile toward our destination.

The Group Covenant is the map to our destination. When each of us agrees to live what the covenant states, we've pushed off from shore and set our sails. Let's see if we can all agree with the expectations of the covenant.

OUR GROUP COVENANT

We all agree to follow the ground rules:

Priority: While we are in this group, we will give the group meetings priority.

Participation: Everyone is encouraged to participate and no one dominates.

Respect: Everyone is given the right to his or her own opinions, and all questions are encouraged and respected.

Confidentiality: Anything that is said in our meetings is never repeated outside the meeting without permission.

Life Change: We will regularly assess our progress toward becoming an authentic community. We will complete any "Taking it Home" activities to reinforce what we are learning and better integrate those lessons into our lives.

Care and Support: Permission is given to call upon each other at any time, especially in times of crisis. The group will provide care for every member.

Accountability: We agree to let the members of our group hold us accountable to commitments we make in whatever loving ways we decide upon. Unsolicited advice giving is not permitted.

Empty Chair: Our group will work together to fill the empty chair with an unchurched person or couple.

Mission: We agree as a group to reach out and invite others to join us, and to work toward multiplication of our group to form new groups.

Ministry: We will encourage one another to volunteer and serve in a ministry, and to support missions work by giving financially and/or personally serving.

I agree to all of the above _____

Date: _____

Record group prayer requests in the space below. In addition to specific prayer requests, ask the group to join you in praying for one another's war zones and for God to help you in finding the right person to fill the empty chair.

Prayer Requests:

Taking it Home

LEADER: Explain that the "Taking it Home" section appears at the end of this session and two others, providing activities to reinforce what the group has discussed.

It will help to have your own Resources Profile completed in advance. Show it to the group and ask them to complete their own profiles and bring them back completed next week. Encourage everyone to complete this assignment before the next session.

Great beginnings foster fantastic endings. We've had a great start! Next week, please come with your Resources Profile completed (see next page).

Sneak Peek

Next time we meet, we're going to have even more fun. A great small group embraces the mosaic God created, displaying the beauty of the diversity that makes up each group. We'll find out how unique we really are and how to unify our diverse group of people to make a strong cord that "is not easily broken."

Scripture Notes

Ecclesiastes 4:9-12

4:9-12 *Two are better than one*. The human solution to life's misery is companionship. Life is much better with a companion or companions, but even with intimate friendship one still experiences the troubles life brings.

MY RESOURCES PROFILE

This session we've touched on the concept that Christian Community means caring for each another 24/7 and includes sharing what we have with one another. The charts below were designed to help you understand your varied resources at this time in your life. Most people think about money and possessions when they think of resources, and these are important. However, our skills, abilities, and time are also vital resources we can share. Knowing each other's unique resources will help your group relate in practical and daily ways. Please complete the inventory below focusing on unique resources that you could share within your group.

My Skills and Abilities	Time	Possessions	Money

Please complete the schedules below. Keep in mind that sometimes schedules must change if you truly want to experience redemptive Christian Community.

My Typical Monday Schedule

Time frame: **Activity:**

_____   _____

_____   _____

_____   _____

_____   _____

_____   _____

_____   _____

_____   _____

_____   _____

My Typical Sunday Schedule

Time frame: **Activity:**

_____   _____

_____   _____

_____   _____

_____   _____

_____   _____

_____   _____

A UNIQUE MOSAIC

UNIFYING OUR GROUP OF DIVERSE PEOPLE

Welcome back! Last week was a lot of fun as we began our journey together and closed by talking and praying for each other's war zones. Even though all of our battles last week probably didn't end with victories, at least we know that we're not alone as we go into each skirmish. Remember, we're here for each other 24/7.

As our ship Small Group heads toward our destination of Christian Community, things of beauty surround us. Yet we realize there is something much more beautiful being fashioned on this trip than these portraits that were carefully designed by the human mind, heart, and hands. God, the greatest artist of all time, created a masterpiece when He placed us together on this excursion. He continues to paint us together on the canvas of His heart. Look from the canvas with me into His eyes and we will see how we bring a smile to the face of God.

 ## BREAKING THE ICE
15 Minutes

> *LEADER: The "Breaking the Ice" questions will help group members get better acquainted. Lead your group to do at least three of the "Breaking the Ice" questions below. Be certain everyone answers questions 3 and 4. Keep the tone of the conversation light and be sure everyone gets a turn.*

1. Who has bragging rights in your group to the following?

   The most dating relationships in high school: _____
   The longest hair as a teenager: _____
   The highest graduating grade point average from high school: _____
   The most athletic during high school: _____
   The high school class clown: _____

2. What was the most daring thing you ever did when you were in high school?

3. A small group has a group dynamic that is made up of the collection of individual member's unique traits. It's like a human body in which every part functions naturally as it should. If you could choose which part of the body you would be for this group, which one would that be and why? Which part would your closest friends say you are?

I'd choose   My friends would say

___	___	Funny Bone – I make people laugh.
___	___	Kidneys – I clean out the bad stuff in other's lives.
___	___	Heart – I pump life into all the other parts of the body.
___	___	Tonsils – I have no vital role; I just enjoy being here.
___	___	Hand – I pick up the pieces when things fall apart.
___	___	Eyes – I guide the group toward its destination.
___	___	Back – I support people through good and bad times.
___	___	Belly Button – I'm not yet sure if I'm in or out.
___		Other: _____

LEADER: *Remind people again of the various resource types (skills and abilities, time, possessions, and money). Then ask each person to tell the group what unique resources he or she discovered that could benefit others in the group. If people are willing, make copies of each person's Resource Profile to distribute to others in the group. Take notes on key resources that are mentioned during your time together.*

4. The way God has shaped each of us provides our group all of the tools it needs to approach every situation confident we can win if we work together. Before this meeting, you completed your Resource Profiles. Let's see what unique resources each of our profiles reveal. Be sure to record each person's unique resources on "Your Group's G-R-I-P Profile" on page 9.

DISCOVERING THE TRUTH   20-25 Minutes

LEADER: *After reading the following introduction, ask someone who didn't read last time to read this week's Scripture passage from Ephesians 4. Be sure to leave at least 15 minutes for the "Connecting" segment at the end of your time together.*

God carefully and artistically painted the most beautiful portrait entitled Christian Community. He exhibits not one, but millions of these masterpieces. The original and perfect masterpiece was in God's gallery before time began. Father, Son, and Holy Spirit are brilliantly portrayed on that particular canvas, the picture-perfect example of Christian Community. Jesus was so overcome by this rendering that, before going to the cross, he prayed this final prayer, "Holy Father, protect them by the power of your name—the name you gave me—so that they may be one as we are on." (John 17:11b NIV). Jesus wants us to be as closely connected to each other as the Trinity is. The Father, Son, and Holy Spirit each exhibit their own personalities, and when all of these personalities are at work, an unparalleled portrait is painted. Jesus Himself longs for our small group to be added to the gallery of groups who have become one in purpose, passion, and life.

We are a mosaic—a multi-faceted, multi-colored montage of past histories, abilities, personalities, and passions. Each of us brings to the group our own unique perspective on life, God-assigned talents, supremely ordained resources, and undying passions to make a difference in the world. Our mosaic can only be formed into a masterpiece if and when each of us allows God to help us realize and live out our own uniqueness in the midst of this diverse, yet connected group. Let's encourage each other to stop trying to be something we're not. Let's focus on being ourselves ... the way God designed us!

Paul recognized how to use the tools of diversity and uniformity to build community. Here's what he wrote to the people in Ephesus who were dealing with the tension of crossing over racial and cultural barriers to form their group.

Paul's Recipe for a Unified Group

[1] I, therefore, the prisoner in the Lord, urge you to walk worthy of the calling you have received, [2] with all humility and gentleness, with patience, accepting one another in love, [3] diligently keeping the unity of the Spirit with the peace that binds [us].
[4] There is one body and one Spirit, just as you were called to one hope [Literally "called in one hope at your calling"]; [5] one Lord, one faith, one baptism, [6] one God and Father of all, who is above all and through all and in all.

Ephesians 4:1-6

LEADER: Discuss as many discovery questions as time permits. The strongest application questions appear in the "Embracing the Truth" section. It will help to highlight in advance the questions you don't want to miss. Familiarize yourself with the Scripture Notes at the end of this session to help clarify any issues.

---

1. Because God made us all so different, it will be an exciting challenge to become a unified group. What are the four characteristics mentioned in verse 2 that we are told to live out so we can accomplish the blending of our diversities? Why do you think each of these is important to building unity?

2. Of the four characteristics mentioned above, which are the most difficult for you to live out? Give an example.

___ **Humility** – the opposite of pride; not thinking of yourself more highly than you ought to

___ **Gentleness** – the opposite of rudeness and harshness; being able to control your emotions

___ **Patience** – never gives up on a relationship; self-restraint that doesn't retaliate quickly

___ **Accepting one another in love** – accepting and loving one another even in the midst of disagreements

3. Do you know someone who exhibits the four characteristics named in question 2? What is your relationship to that person? Describe how you feel about him or her. Describe how you believe other people feel about that person.

4. Verse 3 says, "… diligently keeping the unity of the Spirit with the peace that binds [us]." This means we will in love and tolerate each other even when we have differences. What are some things that prevent people from "keeping the unity of the Spirit with the peace that binds [us]"?

5. Why is it important for Christ-followers to be able to "agree to disagree" without losing respect for each other?

EMBRACING THE TRUTH 10-15 Minutes

LEADER: This section focuses on integrating what group members have learned from the Bible about unity and diversity into their individual lives and small-group philosophy.

1. Have you ever had been a part of a group of people who were supposed to be committed to you but let you down? What was that like for you? Please share this experience with your group.

2. Choose the characteristic from question 2 of "Discovering the Truth" that you tend to struggle with. Share ideas with your group about something practical you can do this week to "exercise" this area of your life.

3. Recall the personal resources you listed in your Resources Profile. Discuss with the group one or two ways that you might be able to practically help or lift up others in this group. How can helping each other develop closeness and unity?

CONNECTING 15 Minutes

LEADER:
Use this "Connecting" time to develop more closeness within your group, as well as to encourage and support one another. Invite everyone to join in and to be open with one another.

It is important to have an apprentice leader in place in the first few weeks. This person can fill in when needed, support the leader, and develop into a future leader who can lead a group when the group multiplies. Be certain an apprentice is in place within the next few weeks.

As a group, we have a unique opportunity to bond as friends and allies. The exciting thing about this bond is that as it transforms our lives as a group, it will begin to power-fully affect other areas of our individual lives as well. Because of this, it is important for us to begin thinking about non-Christian people we know who God may want to touch through this group. At the end of six weeks, we'll be inviting someone to join our group. Use the questions below to set some personal spiritual goals for yourself individually and for the group as a whole.

1. Keeping in mind what we learned in this session, what could each of us do to be certain this group becomes the masterpiece God wants us to become? How can we encourage each other in this group to connect?

2. Write down the first name of someone you know who is not yet a Christian and lives in reasonably close proximity to where you meet. Share this person's name with the group, and ask them to begin praying for him or her this week.

3. What are some specific situations in your life that you would appreciate prayer for now?

Record group prayer requests in the space below. In addition to specific prayer requests, pray together for unity to develop in your group and for the person who will fill the empty chair.

Prayer Requests:

Taking it Home

Finding out each other's resources was more than a fun exercise. Knowing each other's unique resources will help us support and relate to each other better, which will result in greater group unity.

This week we'll complete a Spiritual Gifts Assessment. This exercise will help us unwrap your God-given abilities and skills. We'll use the results of this assessment to help one another reach our full potential individually and as a group.

Sneak Peek

Next time we meet, we'll discover one another's Spiritual Gifts as we continue this journey together. We'll learn how various gifts are designed to work in cooperation just like parts of the body.

Scripture Notes

Ephesians 4:1-6

4:1 I ... urge you. Stylistically, Paul moves from the indicative ("This is the way things are") to the imperative ("This is what must be done").

4:2 humility. Humility is an absence of pride and self-assertion, based upon accurate self-knowledge and on an understanding of the God-given worth of others. Humility is the key to the growth of healthy relationships between people. *gentleness.* Paul is not urging people to be timid and without convictions. Gentleness is the quality of strength under control, like a thoroughbred horse. *patience.* Patience with others is also called long-suffering. *accepting one another.* This is tolerance of the faults of others that springs from humility, gentleness, and patience.

4:4-6 one. Note the emphasis on unity accentuated by the word "one" appearing seven times in these three short verses. Because there is one God, one hope, and one faith ... there should be one body of the Lord's followers unified by His Spirit.

Spiritual Gifts Assessment

Spiritual Gifts ... supernaturally given by God, are His way of making sure no need goes unmet and everyone is effectively influencing those around them. The assessment below was created so you could recognize what spiritual gifts God has given you. This is a fairly comprehensive list of gifts that are held by various churches. Not all churches agree on the list of gifts available to the church today, so talk with your pastor, priest, or minister if you have questions. Check each statement that is true of you. In areas where you check all three of the statements, you most likely have that gift.

Apostleship: The God-given ability to build the foundation for new churches and/or ministries. This gift often relates to church planting or missions work.
___ I find fulfillment in building a ministry from the ground up.
___ I enjoy cultures other than my own.
___ I seem to have a deep desire to reach unreached people in other communities and cultures.

Distinguishing Between Spirits/Discernment: The God-given ability to detect biblical misrepresentations, to make a distinction between right and wrong and good and evil.
___ I find fulfillment in protecting the body of Christ by pointing out when false teaching is taking place, identifying moral and ethical inconsistencies, and by differentiating good from evil.
___ I enjoy pointing out when a statement attributed to God is valid.
___ I seem to have the ability to sense the presence of evil.

Exhortation/Encouragement: The God-given ability to reassure people who are discouraged or vacillating in their faith.
___ I find fulfillment in coming alongside those who are disheartened.
___ I enjoy pointing out the hope found in Scripture to those needing supernatural support.
___ I seem to have the ability to comfort those who are suffering.

Evangelism: The God-given ability to tell non-Christians about Jesus in such a way that they seriously consider starting an eternal relationship with Him.
___ I find fulfillment in telling others about Jesus.
___ I enjoy building friendships with people who don't know Jesus, especially when the goal of the relationship is to help those people start a relationship with Jesus.
___ I seem to have the ability to tell others what Jesus has done in my life without feeling overly nervous or intimidated.

Faith: The God-given ability to believe fully in God's power and to trust God without hesitation to accomplish the promises found in the Bible.
___ I find fulfillment in trusting God to do far beyond that which is possible through human ability.
___ I enjoy building faith in others by unveiling the promises of God to them and encouraging them to trust Him to keep His promises.
___ I seem to have the ability to create an atmosphere of anticipation about what God will do for people.

Giving: The God-given ability to unselfishly give money and resources to individuals in need and to the work of the church.
___ I find fulfillment in meeting tangible needs.
___ I enjoy managing my finances so that I have the means to help others.
___ I seem to have the ability to make money that can be used to meet needs and accomplish ministry.

Healing: The God-given ability to bring emotional, physical, and/or spiritual healing to individuals or groups of people.
___ I find fulfillment in knowing God restores people physically and/or emotionally.
___ I enjoy faithfully walking alongside others as God brings healing to their spirits /bodies.
___ I seem to have the ability to pray for someone and see God do miraculous healing.

Helps: The God-given ability to joyfully accomplish practical tasks that support a ministry or person.
___ I find fulfillment in knowing that the practical things I do free others up to fulfill what God has created them to do.
___ I enjoy serving behind the scenes wherever needed.
___ I seem to have the ability to see great value in carrying out what some would consider insignificant tasks.

Hospitality: The God-given ability to create an environment where people feel welcome and honored.
___ I find fulfillment in making new people feel welcome and valued when they come to a group meeting of any kind.
___ I enjoy preparing my home or a meeting room for guests.
___ I seem to have the ability to notice people who are ill at ease at gatherings, and I am compelled to make them feel welcomed.

Intercession: The God-given ability to passionately pray for people and ministries with extraordinary results.
___ I find fulfillment in knowing that God responds to my prayers.
___ I enjoy pleading to God on behalf of people and ministries.
___ I seem to be energized after praying long periods of time.

Leadership: The God-given ability to obtain and retain followers and to organize, unify, and direct them to accomplish a God-given vision.

__ I find fulfillment in recruiting and guiding people to achieve a common goal.

__ I enjoy telling others what the work we are doing will look like when accomplished.

__ I seem to have the ability to voice a directive, and people respond by doing their parts to complete that directive.

Managing/Administration: The God-given ability to know how a ministry functions, create plans for a ministry, and implement procedures that accomplish the goals of that ministry.

__ I find fulfillment in developing strategies to accomplish work.

__ I enjoy organizing people and tasks to complete a given goal.

__ I seem to have the ability to bring order to organizational disorder.

Mercy: The God-given ability to joyfully meet the emotional and practical needs of those who are suffering.

__ I find fulfillment in being with people in emotional or physical pain.

__ I enjoy meeting the needs of people who are suffering.

__ I seem to have the ability to bring comfort and help to people facing crisis.

Miracles: The God-given ability to make the presence and power of God known through being an instrument to accomplish the miraculous in the name of Jesus.

__ I find fulfillment in believing God will do the miraculous even when those around me question whether He does or will.

__ I enjoy giving God the glory when He uses me to accomplish something beyond human capabilities.

__ I seem to have the ability to articulate a word from God and have it validated by a miraculous outcome.

Prophecy: The God-given ability to discern and boldly reveal truth that rebukes, corrects, and edifies believers and leads to life change and/or repentance.

__ I find fulfillment in knowing that my proclamations to others may keep them from experiencing God's judgment.

__ I enjoy helping others understand God's truth and telling them of the judgment that may come if they do not listen and respond to His expectations.

__ I seem to have the ability to realize and expose sin in others.

Pastoring/Shepherding: The God-given ability to cultivate, protect, and guide people toward spiritual maturity.

__ I find fulfillment in seeing someone transformed from a spiritual babe to maturity.

__ I enjoy modeling Christlike character and I am willing to give my time and energies to see others become more like Him.

__ I seem to have the ability to patiently nurture people toward spiritual maturity.

Teaching: The God-given ability to grasp the truth of God's Word, help others understand it's meaning, and motivate them to apply what has been learned.
___ I find fulfillment in studying the Bible for long periods of time.
___ I enjoy telling others the truth of God's Word knowing it heals and transforms people.
___ I seem to have the ability to verbalize complex truths in easy to understand terms.

Wisdom: The God-given ability to utilize and help others employ God's wisdom to meet a need or accomplish a task.
___ I find fulfillment in applying spiritual and biblical truth in practical ways.
___ I enjoy bringing resolve in the midst of confusion by offering God-given solutions in a given situation.
___ I seem to have the ability to be perceive what is necessary to make the church more effective.

NOTE: The following spiritual gifts have raised a great deal of controversy within the church over the years with regard to definition and usage. Please seek direction from your church leadership and Bible commentaries if you would like to define and assess yourself on these gifts:

- **Tongues (or Languages)**
- **Interpretation of Tongues**
- **Knowledge**

Top Three Gifts I Seem to Have:

1. _____

2. _____

3. _____

Three Gifts I Clearly Do NOT Have:

1. _____

2. _____

3. _____

A Healthy Body

Understanding How Parts of the Body Work Together

Thanks for sharing last week. We're really beginning to see how we fit together as puzzle pieces into God's masterpiece. But, I wonder what would happen if the beautiful image God painted of Christian Community got out of whack? What if a given color in that portrait decided it deserved a more prominent place on the canvas? The masterpiece might become an ugly mess if the color red tried to take over the painting. Instead of this work of art bringing peace to the soul, anger would be the result of its viewing. What if green decided it was the most beautiful color and began to spread itself throughout the piece? Envy would be perceived rather than love and equality. What would be the outcome if yellow concluded it had the right to spread its hue? Cowardice would run across the piece and cause God's powerful work to lose its vigor. This work of art must have balance in order for it to portray what the Great Artist intended.

 ## BREAKING THE ICE   **15 Minutes**

> LEADER: The "Breaking the Ice" questions will relax people and help them continue to connect better with one another. Lead your group to do at least three of the "Breaking the Ice" questions below. Make sure you do the final two icebreakers.

1. To which celebrity would you give "The Most Conceited Person in the World Award"? What did he or she do to earn it?

2. Which position would you choose to play if you were part of a baseball team?
   ___ Player – I love to be in the middle of the action.
   ___ Owner – I enjoy recruiting the right people to create a winning team.
   ___ Coach – I take pleasure in leading the team.
   ___ Assistant Coach – I'll make sure everything is organized and running smoothly.
   ___ Commentator – I love making sure everyone knows what's happening.
   ___ Water Boy – I just want to make sure everyone is comfortable.
   ___ Bat Boy – I'll remove any obstacles that keep the team from scoring.
   ___ Groundskeeper – I'll make sure the field is ready to go.
   ___ Other: _____

3. When you were a younger, were you involved in any accidents that resulted in a particular part of your body being hurt? How did this injury affect what you were able to do?

4. How many of you breathed a sigh of relief when you found out last week that you were made to be a certain way, and that you didn't have to try to be something that you weren't? Would anyone like to share how this knowledge changed the way you lived life last week?

Our time together this week is going to relieve you of even more pressure. Sometimes we think we should be capable of carrying out any tasks asked of us with great expertise. But the Bible is straightforward when it tells us that each person in the church is given specific abilities.

 # DISCOVERING THE TRUTH   20-25 Minutes

Ever wonder where your face would stack up on the "level of importance" totem pole? Right now, glance around the room at the people in your group. If the perspective you have of yourself and your role in the group was based on the totem pole, where do you see yourself in the importance hierarchy? Do you see yourself as being so low on the pole that you simply support the weight of the rest, or do you believe your role is putting pressure on the rest from an elevated position? In all actuality, we all need to turn that pole on its side and recognize that every person in this group is of equal value. Why? Because every role that is God-given carries identical worth.

This week we're going to spend some more time in self-discovery and uncover our spiritual gifts. Spiritual Gifts used in love are the glue that holds Christian Community together. Used together as God intended, they provide the force that enables each person to become all God intended him or her to be.

When Paul wrote 1 Corinthians, he was writing to people who were living in an age when roles were determined by social status. In that culture it was easy for an individual to conclude that his or her responsibility was more important than the responsibilities of others. Holding a high rank in that society signified that a person had achieved some level of importance in the community. Paul blindsided the Corinthians when he wrote them the following letter.

Different but Equal Parts

Narrator:
[12] For as the body is one and has many parts, and all the parts of that body, though many, are one body—so also is Christ. [13] For we were all baptized by one Spirit into one body—whether Jews or Greeks, whether slave or free—and we were all made to drink of one Spirit. [14] So the body is not one part but many. [15] If the foot should say,

Foot:
"Because I am not a hand, I don't belong to the body,'

Narrator:
In spite of this it still belongs to the body. [16] And if the ear should say,

Ear:
"Because I am not an eye, I don't belong to the body,"

Narrator:
In spite of this it still belongs to the body. [17] If the whole body were an eye, where would the hearing be? If the whole were an ear, where would be the sense of smell? [18] But now God has placed the parts, each one of them, in the body just as He wanted. [19] And if they were all the same part, where would the body be? [20] Now, there are many parts, yet one body. [21] So the eye cannot say to the hand,

Eye:
"I don't need you!"

Narrator:
Nor again the head to the feet,

Head:
"I don't need you!"

Narrator:
[22] On the contrary, all the more, those parts of the body that seem to be weaker are

necessary, [23] And those parts of the body that we think to be less honorable, we clothe those with greater honor, and our unpresentable parts have a better presentation, [24] But our presentable parts have no need [of clothing]. Instead, God has put the body together, giving greater honor to the less honorable, [25] so that there would be no division in the body, but that the members would have the same concern for each other.

Narrator, Head, Eye, Ear, and Foot in Unison:
[26] So if one member suffers, all the members suffer with it; if one member is honored, all the members rejoice with it.

1 CORINTHIANS 12:12-26

LEADER: Discuss as many discovery questions as time permits. The strongest application questions appear in the "Embracing the Truth" section, but this section has some application focus. It will help to highlight in advance the questions you don't want to miss. Be sure to leave at least 15 minutes for your "Connecting" time at the end of your session.

---

1. Why would you say that the human body is the perfect illustration of a healthy church?

2. According to verse 18, who determines which role each believer plays in the body of Christ? Read also 1 Corinthians 12:11. What does this verse indicate about whether we select our own spiritual gifts?

3. What happens when one organ of the human body takes over everything or one organ malfunctions?

4. What happens when one organ tries to perform another organ's function? How does it affect the body when somebody is trying to do something they were not made to do? How does it affect the individual?

5. In the church at Corinth, what happened to the people with "weaker ... less honorable ... unpresentable gifts" (vv. 22-23)?

6. In verses 25-26, what does Paul challenge the people, especially those with more spectacular gifts, to do?

 # EMBRACING THE TRUTH   10-15 Minutes

It's time for us to transfer what we have learned about Paul's message to the church in Corinth into our own lives individually and as a group. The fingerprints of the Great Artist are all over this masterpiece of Christian Community. In His wisdom, He has provided through each individual member's gifts everything our group needs to grow which, when you think about it, is truly amazing!

Please take out your Spiritual Gifts Assessment from last week. Then, work through the following questions.

1. Name a time in your life when you tried to do something but failed because you didn't have the ability to accomplish what was asked of you? How did that affect you?

2. Which spiritual gift/gifts does your Spiritual Gifts Assessment lead you to believe you have? Did any of these surprise you? If so, which ones? Why?

3. Take a few moments to write down each group member's primary spiritual gift(s) on "Your Group's G-R-I-P Profile" on page 9.

CONNECTING

LEADER: Use the "Connecting" time to develop a sense of community in your group, as members continue to share and build one another up. Encourage everyone to join in and be open with one another. Pass out a 3 x 5" card to each person in the group. Remind everyone about the purpose of the empty chair.

Remember, as we grow together in community, we want to reach out to others too. The empty chair is our reminder that we need to invite others. At the end of our *Great Beginnings* study, we will be asking someone to join us as a group member. The amazing thing is that we will be sharing Christ with this person simply through our actions as we do life together as a group, as we live out authentic Christian Community!

1. On the 3 x 5" card you've been given, write down the name of a person you know who doesn't have a relationship with Jesus Christ ... someone you would like to see fill our empty chair. Let's place all of these cards on the empty chair during our meetings over the next three weeks. Let's take a minute right now to pray together. You'll want to pray specifically for the person whose name you wrote down on your card.

2. As we prepare to close our discussion of a healthy "body" or group, what do you think might happen within our small group if one person takes over and/or someone else doesn't carry out his God-given role?

3. What are some ways that you can use your spiritual gift/gifts to help the people in our group?

4. One at a time, have the group members pray briefly for each person. Pray that God would reveal more about his or her spiritual gift(s). Pray for one another's personal life situations, the courage to use your spiritual gifts for one another, and the courage to allow others to help each of you.

Take a few minutes to share any other prayer needs. Record those group prayer requests in the space below and pray regularly for them between now and the next session.

Prayer Requests:

Taking it Home

LEADER: *"Taking it Home" this week asks group members to think of specific ways they can utilize their spiritual gift(s) to help someone else in the group. Encourage everyone to fill in the blanks provided with the name of a person and an idea before they leave today and to finish the project before the next session.*

It is important to remember that the spiritual gift/gifts that we've been given are for the benefit of others and the church; they are not for ourselves. This week's "Taking it Home" exercise is going to ask you to use the gift/gifts God has given you to help someone else in your group. Be creative, be flexible, and be proactive with this project! If you can't think of any way to use your gift/gifts for someone else, then ask the group (or group leader) right now to help you come up with something. Have fun as you see how God uses you to encourage or build up someone else!

Write on the line below the name of the person in your group you will focus on this week and your idea of how you will serve them by using your spiritual gift/gifts. Make sure you do this before you leave the meeting! And work to finish your project this week.

_____

This is getting to be really fun! Thanks for sharing each week. Just knowing we'll be together again is encouragement for the rest of the week. Remember, this mosaic of Christian Community can't be completed without you!

SNEAK PEEK

Next time we meet, we'll do one of the coolest exercises of all. You don't want to miss this one!

SCRIPTURE NOTES

1 CORINTHIANS 12:12-26

12:12 is one and has many parts. This is Paul's central point in verses 12-30: "diversity within unity." So also is Christ. The church is the body of Christ (v. 27), and so indeed Christ can be understood to be made up of many parts. Yet He is also the Lord (v. 3), and thus head over that church.

12:15-26 Having established that all Christians are part of one body (which is, in fact, Christ's body) and that this body has a variety of parts, Paul makes two primary points: there are a variety of gifts (vv. 15-20), and each gift is vital, regardless of its nature (vv. 21-26).

TRANSFORMING TALES

SHARING OUR STORIES AND LIVES

Every sailing vessel has a past. She may have survived treacherous storms or navigated dangerous straits. She may have transported precious cargo in her hold or carried hopeful passengers to exotic shores. We resemble these glorious ships. She has a past and so do each of us. She has a story ... so do we. The more we know of our pasts, the more we can gain from each other as we sail together into Christian Community. On this journey, one of the gifts we can give each other is our stories.

 ## BREAKING THE ICE   15 Minutes

> *LEADER: These "Breaking the Ice" questions are designed to encourage group members to share more of their personal stories. Answer at least three of the icebreakers below, making sure that everyone answers the last two.*

1. Briefly share an embarrassing high school experience that you would most like to forget.

2. Describe the most menial or mundane job you've ever had. What did you like or dislike about this position?

3. If you could get a "do over" on one era of your life, which would you choose and why?
   ___ Preschool
   ___ Grade School
   ___ High School
   ___ College
   ___ Early Adulthood
   ___ Later Adulthood

> *LEADER: Encourage each person to share a key insight from last week's "Taking it Home" assignment.*

4. How did your "Taking it Home" assignment go? How did you respond as someone served you using a spiritual gift? What was your experience like as you exercised your own spiritual gift last week for someone else?

We're going to have lots of opportunities to use our spiritual gifts and our past experiences to grow one another. During group time, feel free to exercise your spiritual gifts, use your unique resources, and/or share your past experiences. Doing so will help each of us reach our full potential. Also, we'll make a huge difference in one another's lives if we'll do this for each other when we're away from our group meetings too.

 # DISCOVERING THE TRUTH 20-25 Minutes

If you think about it, your story is His (God's) story. It's an account that, even though sometimes tangled and difficult to divulge, opens the door so that we can enter into Christian Community. As we journey into this jungle, we'll need to use the machete of safe haven to cut away at the high grass of self-consciousness. We must open our mouths and allow our voices to narrate our story, His story. The only way to arrive at connectedness is to know one another, really. And the first step toward truly knowing one another is self-disclosure. In the weeks and months ahead, we'll do this by revealing our history with one another at a pace that is carefully chosen and a speed that should be comfortable for all.

Today we're going to crack the door into one another's lives as we begin to share some of our own spiritual journeys. Now, don't sweat it if you have some less than desirable moments in your account. You're not alone. Check out one of God's most potent church leaders, Paul, as he exposes his past and his journey with Jesus.

A Redemptive Story

LEADER: Tonight's study should be focused on people telling their stories rather than on learning about Paul's. Spend a few minutes using the questions to help your group prepare to do the exercise that follows. It will help to have your spiritual journey mapped out prior to arriving at the meeting. Be sure to leave at least 15 minutes for "Connecting" at the end of the session.

[12] I give thanks to Christ Jesus our Lord, who has strengthened me, because He considered me faithful, appointing me to the ministry— [13] one who was formerly a blasphemer, a persecutor, and an arrogant man. Since it was out of ignorance that I had acted in unbelief, I received mercy, [14] and the grace of our Lord overflowed, along with the faith and love that are in Christ Jesus.

¹⁵ This saying is trustworthy and deserving of full acceptance: "Christ Jesus came into the world to save sinners"—and I am the worst of them. ¹⁶ But I received mercy because of this, so that in me, the worst [of them], Christ Jesus might demonstrate the utmost patience as an example to those who would believe in Him for eternal life. ¹⁷ Now to the King eternal, immortal, invisible, the only God, be honor and glory for ever and ever. Amen.

1 TIMOTHY 1:12-17

1. What did you learn about Paul because he told his story?

2. What did you learn about Jesus because Paul told his story?

3. How does hearing Paul's story help you in sharing your own?

God uses our experiences, good and bad, to make us more like Him. When we tell our stories, God uses them to help others through hard times of their own. The Bible is right on when it reminds us that, "We know that all things work together for the good of those who love God: those who are called according to His purpose" (Romans 8:28).

Mapping Our Spiritual Journeys

Today we're going to do something really exciting! You may have wondered why your book has a mostly empty page. That page is there because we're going to draw our spiritual journey and then share it with the group. Here's how this works. Each of you will use the crayons provided to create a picture that maps out your spiritual journey. Some of you may draw a roadmap with stops or speed traps identified along the way to represent your journey. Some of you may depict a mountain you've been climbing indicating where the shortcuts are that you've found that have made the journey easier. Don't sweat your inability to create a masterpiece. Anything you create will be fine. Use your imagination!

LEADER: Model the assignment for the group by showing them your drawing and share your story before you ask them to complete this exercise. NOTE: Make sure you've brought enough crayons and large sheets of paper with you for the whole group. If you don't have large sheets of paper, use the next page in the book. Allow only 10 minutes for drawing the maps.

YOUR SPIRITUAL JOURNEY

As you draw out your spiritual journey, be creative. Focus on your individual experiences, the events that have shaped you, and your passions in life. Include the birth of dreams, the death of dreams, losses, experiences that have forced you to grow, turning points, and major milestones. You'll have about 10 minutes for this experience.

EMBRACING THE TRUTH

> *LEADER: This next activity gives each group member an opportunity to briefly share his or her Spiritual Journey Map. Make sure that each person is affirmed after sharing. Also, make sure the group gets a chance to ask questions about anything that was unclear in the presentation before you move on to the next person.*

We can't begin to really know each other until we truly understand the experiences (both good and bad) that have shaped us into the people we are today, as well as the dreams and passions that God has implanted in us. As you hear people in our group share, you will inevitably witness mighty evidence of God's grace, mercy, and love. By taking part in this experience, you will move your relationship with this group to a whole new level. IMPORTANT: Make sure to treasure and protect the stories that you are about to be entrusted with.

One by one, share your drawing and tell your story. Make sure you ask if anyone has questions at the end of your story. Be sure to record each person's unique experiences and passions on "Your Group's G-R-I-P Profile" on page 9.

 # CONNECTING

15 Minutes

> *LEADER: Laying hands on someone and praying for them may be new for some of your group members. Remind the group that the people touching them simply want them to know the warmth that comes from God. Laying hands on a person is a way to let that person know that you want to share the burden that individual is presently carrying alone. Be sensitive. Some people may not want others to touch them, but would still welcome a prayer being voiced on their behalf.*

1. Lay hands on and pray specifically for those members whose experiences may still cause them pain.

2. Pray about any other concerns the group members may have.

3. Ask if anyone has felt compelled to invite the person whose name he or she wrote down last week and placed on the empty chair. If someone has, ask the group to pray for the courage necessary to make that contact. Tell the group this person will be invited to join the group in a few short weeks.

Prayer Requests:

Sneak Peek

This week you have turned an important corner in developing closeness within your group. Next time we meet, we'll discuss a list that will radically change the relationships you have with your kids, your friends, your boyfriend or girlfriend, your spouse, and even the people in this group.

Scripture Notes

Romans 8:28

8:28 all things work together. It is God who takes that which is adverse and painful (the groans, the persecution, and even death—vv. 35-36) and brings profit out of it. *for the good of those who love God.* This does not mean things work out so that believers preserve their comfort and convenience. Rather, such action on God's part enables these difficult experiences to assist in the process of salvation and growth. *those who love God: who are called according to His purpose.* The love people have for God is a reflection of the fact and reality of God's love for them as expressed in His call to individuals to follow Christ. A person's love for God has been said to be a proof of God's love for that person. If God had not called an individual, that person would still be His enemy, unable and unwilling to love Him.

1 Timothy 1:12-17

1:12-17 blasphemer ... persecutor ... arrogant man. Paul was a well-respected Jewish leader and a passionate persecutor of the new sect of faithful Christ-followers. He was actually responsible for killing Christians. God in His amazing grace and mercy transformed Paul from a Christ-hater to the greatest evangelist of all time for the kingdom of Christ.

LIFE TOGETHER ... REALLY

DISCOVERING THE POWER OF COMMUNITY

What an awesome get together last week! Did you notice ... no homework? All of us are working through some kinds of issues in our lives. I hope those of you who were dealing with some stuff from your past have started praying for God's help and healing in those areas. Not only that, I hope you realize that all of us are here to lend a hand as you go through the process. We would like to put our spiritual gifts, past experiences, and resources to use for your benefit. Someday you'll look over your shoulder and spot your present wounds in your rearview mirror as you speed away at a pace so fast they can never catch up with you. At that point, you'll be doing life with all the gusto God intended. When that happens, we're all going to celebrate with you.

 ## BREAKING THE ICE   15 Minutes

> LEADER: These "Breaking the Ice" questions are designed to encourage group members to share more of their personal stories and to begin to evaluate what they value. Answer at least two of the icebreakers below making sure you don't skip the last one.

1. When you were growing up, what is the most mischievous prank you and a group of friends played on someone? Who instigated the prank? What was your role in that prank?

2. If you could be part of one of the teams listed below, which would you choose and why?
   ___ Volleyball – Every player gets to play every position.
   ___ Baseball – You get three strikes and you're out, but you still get to bat again.
   ___ Hockey – I love a good fight!
   ___ Football – Someone else calls the plays.
   ___ Boxing – I'm a rugged individualist.
   ___ Cheerleader – I enjoy encouraging others on to greatness.
   ___ Basketball – Every player has to perform his or her part correctly for the play to succeed.
   ___ Other: _____

3. What is your most prized material possession? How did you acquire it? What is it worth to you?

DISCOVERING THE TRUTH 20-25 Minutes

We've finished four weeks on the voyage to Christian Community. We've gone ashore at the islands of Resources Recognition, Spiritual Gift Appreciation, and His Story Recollection. Now we're about to dock at the next to last stop of our journey, the island of Small Group Essentials. This island offers clues that will help us reach true Christian Community. Once we unearth these clues, we'll have a few more of the necessary tools for building community.

In this session, we're going to dig up the primary practices that will allow us to get to Christian Community. Before we unpack the crucial Scripture passage for this session, I want to reveal an important list to you. The Bible is full of "one anothers." These actions, when lived out between group members, become the compass that directs us to Christian Community. Let's read them aloud.

LEADER: Ask a different person to read the list in each of the categories below.

Love Each Other:
1. to fulfill God's law (Romans 13:8)
2. to increase our love for one another (2 Thessalonians 1:3)
3. to overflow in love for one another (1 Thessalonians 3:12)
4. to cover a multitude of sins (1 Peter 4:8)

Connect with Each Other in Integrity:
1. to fellowship with one another (1 John 1:7)
2. to forgive one another (Ephesians 4:32; Colossians 3:13)
3. to greet one another with healthy touch (Romans 16:16; 1 Corinthians 16:20; 2 Corinthians 13:12; 1 Peter 5:14)
4. to wait for one another to break bread (1 Corinthians 11:33)
5. to help one another through difficult times (1 Corinthians 12:26)

Serve Each Other:

1. to use our spiritual gifts (1 Peter 4:10)
2. to love, relinquishing our freedom when necessary (Galatians 5:13)
3. to show kindness and pursue what is good for one another (1 Thessalonians 5:15)
4. to show concern for one another (1 Corinthians 12:25)
5. to carry one another's burdens (Galatians 6:2)
6. to show honor as you "wash one another's feet" (John 13:14)
7. to work with one another (1 Corinthians 3:9; 2 Corinthians 6:1)

Teach Each Other:

1. to teach and admonish one another (Colossians 3:16)
2. to instruct and model Jesus to one another (Romans 15:14)

Encourage Each Other:

1. to encourage one another to avoid deception and live for Christ (Hebrews 3:13; Hebrews 10:25)
2. to speak the truth to one another (Ephesians 4:25)
3. to lay down our lives for one another (1 John 3:16)
4. to spur one another on to love and good works (Hebrews 10:24)

Build Up Each Other:

1. to strengthen one another in tough times (1 Thessalonians 4:18 and 5:11)
2. to share a psalm, a teaching, or a revelation (1 Corinthians 14:26)

Meet Each Other's Spiritual Needs:

1. to confess our sins one to another (James 5:16)
2. to pray for one another (James 5:16)

Live a Life of Humility Toward Each Other:

1. to honor others above yourself (Romans 12:10)
2. to be in agreement or of the same mind one with each other (2 Corinthians 13:11; Romans 12:16 and 15:5)
3. to not criticize or judge one another (Romans 14:13; James 4:11)
4. to not complain or speak badly of one another (James 5:9)
5. to submit to one another (Ephesians 5:21)
6. to be clothed with humility toward one another (1 Peter 5:5)

Live in Harmony with Each Other:

1. to be patient with one another (Ephesians 4:2)
2. to live in peace one with another (Mark 9:50)
3. to accept and welcome one another with hospitality (Romans 15:7; 1 Peter 4:9)
4. to glorify God together (Romans 15:6)

This is an amazing list, but these aren't the only biblical qualities that are necessary for living in Christian Community. There are four other biblical essentials that are required. In the Book of Acts, after the early believers received the Holy Spirit at Pentecost, Peter preached, and 3,000 people accepted Christ! Guess what the earliest Christian leaders did then? They put these brand new believers into small groups. And when they did they saw amazing results. Check it out!

A Perfect Model

[42] And they devoted themselves to the apostles' teaching, to fellowship, to the breaking of bread, and to prayers. [43] The fear came over everyone, and many wonders and signs were being performed through the apostles. [44] Now all the believers were together and had everything in common. [45] So they sold their possessions and property and distributed the proceeds to all, as anyone as anyone had a need. [46] And every day they devoted themselves [to meeting] together in the temple complex, and broke bread from house to house. They ate their food with gladness and simplicity of heart, [47] praising God and having favor with all the people. And every day the Lord added to them those who were being saved.

ACTS 2:42-47

LEADER: Answer as many of the discovery questions as time permits. Be certain to discuss questions 3, 6, and 7. Be sure to leave time for the "Embracing the Truth" and "Connecting" sections.

---

1. What does the word "devoted" mean to you?

2. Which group of people or cause would you say you have been completely devoted to? What sacrifices have you made to achieve this full devotion?

3. What are the four things these Christ-followers devoted themselves to in verse 42?

4. On a scale of 1 to 10, how devoted are you at this point to each of these 4 directives?

5. According to verse 45, what did these Christ-followers do when someone was in need?

6. What was the level of commitment of these Christ-followers to each other and their mission? Why do you think they had this attitude?

7. What was the outcome of these Christ-followers sharing their lives in these small groups (v. 47)? How do you think the general population who saw the way the early Christians were living would have described the relationships these Christians had with each other?

8. How would you describe those relationships?

So, you can see that a small group done in the right way can have a radical impact. A group that builds itself upon the early church's model will be committed to the Lord and to each other. This deep love for God and each other will touch and change people. It will have a profound influence on the world!

EMBRACING THE TRUTH

> *LEADER: This section focuses on helping group members integrate what they have learned from the Bible about their small-group essentials into their personal lives.*

A group that isn't made up of strong relationships won't exist for long. As humans, we long for close, intimate, life-changing relationships. It is what we were created for! Yet, so many people live unconnected lives longing to be truly known by others. The beauty of a small group is that it provides the setting for what happened so long ago in the early church to happen again today.

1. What is appealing to you about the kind of friendships described in Acts chapter 2?

2. Of the list below, check off the top three things that you be willing to give up so that this group could experience Christian Community.
   ___ Time
   ___ Money
   ___ Possessions
   ___ My Comfort Zone
   ___ Personal Biases
   ___ My "I can do it myself" lifestyle
   ___ Other:

3. Looking at the above list, which item is the easiest for you to sacrifice? Which is the most difficult for you to surrender? Why? _____

CONNECTING:

15 Minutes

Pretty deep stuff! Christian Community is the most meaningful place to live. But like anything of great worth, it requires something from us.

> *LEADER: Be very sensitive as you lead your group to exchange a personal possession. If the members of your group don't have something with them they can exchange, complete this exercise next week. The important thing to remember is this: We are helping the group learn to give to others even when it is something of worth. Don't allow your group to purchase something new to give away next week. Ask them to exchange things that have meaning to them. Model this first for the group by giving away a personal item that you have brought.*

1. Let's do something pretty amazing. Let's break the barrier of self-gratification and give something away. Each person should take something that they have in their possession at this time and give it to another group member. As you hand it to them, tell them what it is, where you received it, and why it is special to you. Keep the item you receive as a reminder of the need to sacrifice for one another throughout the life of this group.

2. Pray together that each group member will make the necessary sacrifices so the group can experience Christian Community. Also, pray for people who are continuing on the journey toward wholeness and for the group's apprentice since he or she will start helping out in a few short weeks. Finally, pray for the person who will fill the empty chair. Be sure to tell the person who is inviting this individual to connect with them in the upcoming week. In a few weeks, you will want them to attend.

Record group prayer requests in the space below and pray regularly for them between now and the next session.

Prayer Requests:

Sneak Peek

Next time we meet, we'll wrap up our first six weeks as a group with a very special event.

SCRIPTURE NOTES

ACTS 2:42-47

2:42 devoted themselves. The four components of the church's life here may represent what occurred at their gatherings. *teaching.* The foundation for the church's life was the instruction given by the apostles as the representatives of Jesus. *fellowship.* Literally, "sharing." While this may include the aspect of sharing to meet material needs (v. 45), it most likely refers to their common participation in the Spirit as they worshipped together (1 Cor. 12). *the breaking of bread.* The Lord's Supper in which they remembered His death (Luke 22:19) and recognized His presence among them (Luke 24:30-31). *prayers.* This may refer to set times and forms of prayer—the typical practice of the Jews.

2:43-47 The picture of the church is one of continual growth (v. 47) marked by generous sharing (vv. 44-45) and by joyful worship and fellowship (vv. 46-47). The worship at the temple continued as before since the line dividing Christianity from Judaism had not yet been drawn. Christians simply saw their faith as the natural end of what the Jewish faith had always declared.

2:44-45 everything in common. The shared life that these early Christians practiced was simply an outgrowth of the intense love people had for each other through Jesus Christ. They believed that in Christ each person's need should in some sense become everyone's need. This attitude is a key component to authentic Christian Community today as well.

COMMUNITY UNLEASHED

CONTINUING THE ADVENTURE ...

Last week was another great time together. I don't know about you, but my prayers about the sacrifices I need to make to be more devoted to this group were difficult to pray. There's so much I'm forced to be dedicated to; I'm evaluating what changes I'm going to have to make so that I can be as devoted as God wants me to be to Him and this group. Maybe you're in the same boat. This is something I'll continue to work on during the months we're together because I'm committed to arriving with you at our destination of Christian Community. If we all are committed, this trip will be the time of our lives.

 ## BREAKING THE ICE   10-15 Minutes

> LEADER: Tell the group this is the last session of your first study, which is designed to help them know how they can help each other grow spiritually. Mention that the group will begin a new study the next time you meet. Choose at least two of the three icebreakers below to engage with your group. Make sure everyone answers the final question.

1. Did your parents ever tell you, "Wait until you're older; you'll understand then"? Explain an instance from your life where you now know this advice to be true.

2. If you could choose any person in the world to mentor you, who would that person be? Why would you choose that person?

3. Of the list below, which person would you most like to influence and why?
   ___ My teenager – making some bad decisions
   ___ My child's teacher – not sure how to do the job
   ___ My parents – didn't have life training themselves when it was most needed
   ___ My boss – needs to understand the employees' situations better
   ___ My best friend – is out of control!
   ___ _____ – is gifted and could accomplish greater things with help
   ___ Other: _____

▼ DISCOVERING THE TRUTH 20-25 Minutes

Here we are at our final destination, the Isle of Christian Community. On this journey, we've collected the tools we need to live on this island .We are about to go ashore, but to really experience it, but we're going to have to stay a while.

As our ship enters the bay, we roll into a concert. People are dancing, singing, and enjoying life. No one seems to be alone. Everyone seems connected on these exotic shores. The entire group is holding signs high above their heads welcoming us to their isle of elation. Some of the signs reveal clues about the holder's personal story. One reads, "Found Jesus Here!" Another says, "Sweeter than the Big Apple." Another delivers this thought provoking message, "Still Struggling, But No Longer Alone." A creative type holds this descriptive declaration, "Colors Beyond Comprehension." But my personal favorite simply reads, "Wouldn't Go Back!" Some of these beach dwellers seem to have come to shore with baggage that has been replaced by peace of mind and lifelong friendships. Others, who were obviously burned by life, now have a healthy, healed, and hopeful future. We are overjoyed as we walk barefoot in the sand with the sun warming our faces. Returning to our lonelier world and substandard life is no longer an option.

Experiencing Christian Community, as you have concluded by now, demands more from us than just attending meetings. It requires a heart connection between group members as well as a personal transformation and the ongoing redemptive work of the Holy Spirit. Without personal transformation the group cannot reach deep heart connection. Only when we become more like Christ can we connect with each other in truly fantastic ways. So, we're going to end our first six weeks of group life discovering how we can be transformed individually and how the group can assist in that process.

Renovation 101: Required Tool List

LEADER: Ask a different person to read each of the following passages. Be sure to leave at least 15 minutes for the "Connecting" segment at the end of your time together.

[16] All Scripture is inspired by God and is profitable for teaching, for rebuking, for correcting, for training in righteousness, [17] so that the man of God may be complete, equipped for every good work.

2 TIMOTHY 3:16-17

Iron sharpens iron, and one man sharpens another.

PROVERBS 27:17

[11] And He personally gave some to be apostles, some prophets, some evangelists, some pastors and teachers, [12] for the training of the saints in the work of ministry, to build up the body of Christ [13] until we all reach unity in the faith and in the knowledge God's Son, [growing] into a mature man with a stature measured by Christ's fullness.

EPHESIANS 4:11-13

[2] Consider it a great joy, my brothers, whenever you experience various trials, [3] knowing that the testing of your faith produces endurance. [4] But endurance must do its complete work, so that you may be mature and complete, lacking nothing.

JAMES 1:2-4

[7] Rather, train yourself in godliness, [8] for, the training of the body has a limited benefit, but godliness is beneficial in every way, since it holds promise for the present life and also for the life to come.

1 TIMOTHY 4:7B-8

LEADER: There is a long list of questions between this section and the next. You know your group well enough now to recognize which questions will be most appropriate for them. Answer as many as time will allow. The strongest application questions appear in the "Embracing the Truth" section. It will help to highlight in advance the questions you don't want to miss.

---

1. Each of the passages above reveals one tool used by God to renovate a person's heart. Name the five tools God uses to transform us. Remember, you'll find one in each of the passages above.

   _____   _____

   _____   _____

   _____

2. In 2 Timothy 3:16-17, what does "teaching, rebuking, correcting, and training in righteousness" mean? What do these things prepare us for?

3. Do you know someone who has really allowed the Bible to shape his or her life? Describe the attitudes and actions that this person portrays that lead you to believe the Bible is his or her guide for life?

4. How has the Bible shaped our generation's view of life and the lifestyle we should live? How has it shaped you personally?

5. Have you ever been involved in an activity where you were required to complete certain tasks for the team to be successful? Explain the activity. Describe what you were personally held accountable for.

___ Sports Team:

___ Academic Team:

___ Ministry Team:

___ Leadership Team:

___ Speech Team:

___ Singing or Drama Team:

___ Other:

6. According to James 1:2–4, we are to be joyful even during difficult times. Why is it hard to be joyful when the trials of life blindside us? Is there a difference between being joyful *for* the trials and being joyful *in* the trials? If so, what is the difference?

7. How can each of us help one another grow in our faith during hard times instead of losing our faith? According to verse 4, what is the outcome of finding God in the midst of our adversity?

8. Name the spiritual disciplines you think all Christ-followers should be involved in?

▌▲ EMBRACING THE TRUTH   10-15 Minutes

> LEADER: *This section focuses on encouraging group members to identify spiritual disciplines that they will commit to carry out for the benefit of the group.*

1. Why are people sometimes hesitant to be held accountable? What keeps you from wanting accountability in your life?

2. Think about how spiritual gifts are used between group members to build one another up. If someone in our small group was going through a divorce, how would someone with the gift of mercy use that gift to build up that person? What about the gifts of teaching, helps, leadership, or other gifts?

3. Which of the five tools you found in the Bible passages above has God used most in your life to date? How has it helped or changed you?

4. For you to become all that God wants you to become and for our group to truly become a Christian Community, it's going to take some work on your part. Which of the spiritual disciplines will you commit to carry out? Would you like to be held accountable? If so, who would you like to be accountable to?

 # CONNECTING

15 Minutes

LEADER: This final "Connecting" time will involve a very special commissioning ceremony for your group. As you spend time commissioning one another, remind group members that to commission someone is to empower that person to accomplish what he or she is being commissioned to do. Remind them that they are being commissioned to use all the tools discussed over the last six sessions to make this group all it is meant to be.

As we continue together in our group, we'll want to be certain we use all that we have discovered on our journey together to help one another grow. Commission one another for the part each of you will play in the group by standing in a circle and holding hands. The leader and/or apprentice should pray specifically for each member in the group by name. Feel free to lay hands on each individual as they are being prayed for.

LEADER: Give group members the opportunity to reflect together on the last six weeks. Ask volunteers to share what they've learned and how they plan to integrate this learning into their lives. Take a few minutes before you close this final session to discuss how your group will continue, so you can carry on within this community of friends as you continue to move toward a truly redemptive Christian Community.

1. For six weeks, we've shared an intimate and unique experience. Look back over the life of this study and evaluate your journey. Where were you at the beginning of this journey? How has living in Christian Community affected your life?

2. Take turns sharing favorite memories from your time together. What will you never forget?

3. Look ahead to the future of your group and decide how you will continue living together in Christian Community. When will you meet again? What will you study? Review "Where do we go from here?" on the next page to facilitate your discussion.

4. Record prayer requests in the space below. Pray for the future direction of the group and for the person who will invite the individual to fill the empty chair in your next meeting. Make sure you spend some time thanking God for the invaluable friendships you have made and the lessons you have learned throughout this experience.

Prayer Requests:

YOUR JOURNEY TOGETHER HAS ONLY BEGUN ...

WHERE DO WE GO FROM HERE?

Check the types of studies that you find most interesting:
____ Spiritual growth and development
____ Life and message of Jesus
____ Personal development, such as managing stress, developing relationships, enhancing marriage, etc.
____ Major truths of the Christian faith
____ Teaching of the Apostle Paul
____ Books from the New Testament other than the Gospels and Letters of Paul
____ Stories and teaching from the Old Testament
____ Areas of personal struggle; recovering from grief, broken relationships, addictions, divorce, etc.
____ Student-focused issues and teaching
____ Other: _____

Of the various study series listed below, check those that would benefit your group or that you'd be interested in personally.

For information on the latest series and studies, visit www.SerendipityHouse.com or call 800-525-9563.

____ Foundations of the Faith series
____ Understanding the Savior series
____ Message of Paul series
____ Words of Faith series (various New Testament books)
____ HomeWorks series (marriage and family)
____ Growing in Christ series
____ Picking Up the Pieces series (recovery and healing)
____ Fellowship Church series (various biblical and topical studies)
____ Life Connections® series (various biblical and topical studies with a master-teacher format, so it works well as an alternative to traditional Sunday School)
____ Men of Purpose (men of the Bible)
____ Other: _____

Students ...
____ Flood series (DVD-driven studies for youth meetings)
____ Hang Time series (life's tough issues)
____ God Talk series (Christian beliefs)
____ Life Connections® Youth series (based on the adult Life Connections® series)
____ Foundations of the Faith series
____ Fellowship Church series (various biblical and topical studies)

LEADER NOTES

General Tips:

1. Prepare for each meeting by reviewing the material, praying for each group member, asking the Holy Spirit to join you at each meeting, and making Jesus the centerpiece of every experience.
2. Create the right environment by making sure chairs are arranged so each person can see the eyes of every other attendee. Set the room temperature at 69 degrees. Make sure pets are in a location where they cannot interrupt the meeting. Request that cell phones are turned off unless someone is expecting an emergency call. Have music playing as people arrive (volume low enough for people to converse) and, if possible, burn a sweet-smelling candle.
3. Try to have soft drinks and coffee available for early arrivals.
4. Have someone with the spiritual gift of hospitality ready to make any new attendees feel welcome.
5. Be sure there is adequate lighting so that everyone can read without straining.
6. There are four types of questions during each session: Observation (What is the passage telling us?), Interpretation (What does the passage mean?), Self-revelation (How am I doing in light of the truth unveiled?), and Application (Now that I know what I know, what will I do to integrate this truth into my life?). You won't able to use all the questions in each study, but be sure to use some from each of these types of questions.
7. Connect with group members away from group time. The amount of participation you have during your group meetings is directly related to the amount of time you connect with your group members away from the meeting time.
8. Don't get impatient about the depth of relationship group members are experiencing. Building real Christian Community takes time.
9. Be sure pens and/or pencils are available for attendees at each meeting.
10. Never ask someone to pray aloud without first getting their permission.

Every Meeting:

1. Before the icebreakers, do not say, "Now we're going to do an icebreaker." The meeting should feel like a conversation from beginning to end, not a classroom experience.
2. Be certain every member responds to the icebreaker questions. The goal is for every person to hear his or her own voice early in the meeting. People will then feel comfortable to converse later on. If members can't think of a response, let them know you'll come back to them after the others have spoken.
3. Remember, a great group leader talks less than 10% of the time. If you ask a question and no one answers, just wait. If you create an environment where you fill the gaps of silence, the group will quickly learn they needn't join you in the conversation.
4. Don't be hesitant to call people by name as you ask them to respond to questions or to give their opinions. Be sensitive, but engage everyone in the conversation.
5. Don't ask people to read aloud unless you have gotten their permission prior to the meeting. Feel free to ask for volunteers to read.

Session 1 Tips:

1. Committing to the covenant may be difficult for some attendees. Your group may need time to think about and pray about this. Give members time to take the covenant home with them and review it if necessary. The group can commit as a whole during an upcoming session. However, be sure the whole group agrees to the covenant.
2. Explain the "empty chair" concept, which is part of the covenant, as follows: "This empty chair will remain unfilled only until one of us invites a person who is separated from God to become a part of our group. As the group interacts, the guest will realize Jesus is real and will step toward faith in Him."
3. During snack time, have group members pass their books to one another to write names, addresses, e-mail contacts, phone numbers in the Group Directories (p. 4).
4. Be sure you explain to the group how to do the Resources Profile.

Session 2 Tips:

1. Begin looking for a member who would make a good apprentice. When you speak with the group, carefully outline what the term apprentice means. This is a heavy responsibility. Talk to good candidates individually.
2. Be certain you show the group your completed Spiritual Gifts Assessment, and then explain to the group members how to do their own.

Session 3 Tips:

1. Be sure you have enough 3 x 5" cards for each member at this meeting. If possible, call or e-mail the group members sometime during the week and encourage them to use their spiritual gift/gifts to help someone else in the group.
2. If your group is struggling to get answers for the first two "Discovering the Truth" questions, some ideas are listed below:

What did you learn about Paul because he told his story?
- He is a thankful person.
- He has a friendship with Jesus.
- He draws his strength from Christ.
- He has been appointed to the serve Christ.
- He was a blasphemer and persecutor. He was a violent person.
- He was shown mercy by God. He received a lot of grace.
- At one point in his lifetime, he was an unbeliever.
- He considered himself the worst of sinners.
- We have nothing to be ashamed of because we are not who we used to be.

What did you learn about Jesus because Paul told his story?
- Jesus deserves thanks for my changed life.
- Jesus is the One to ask for strength.
- Jesus is the One who calls us.
- Faith and love are found in Jesus.
- Jesus came to save sinners. Jesus shows mercy to us.
- Jesus reveals Himself to others through our changed lives.

Session 4 Tips:

1. Be sure to share your own Spiritual Journey Map before group members begin to draw their own. You'll need to draw your spiritual journey on paper before the group arrives.
2. Have enough crayons or markers so the entire group to be able to color at one time.
3. Be sensitive. Don't push someone to share information he or she is not ready to divulge at this point in the life of the group.

Session 5 Tips:

1. Ask group members to copy or cut out the pages listing the "one anothers." Suggest these are put on a refrigerator door or someplace where they are consistently visible.
2. When you get to the exercise of exchanging something between members, be sure the members know that this is something they are sacrificing that will not be returned to the owner. It is a gift to be kept forever.
3. Make sure you've chosen an item to give and a person to give it to before this meeting. Model this exchange for your group. Then ask the group to take turns doing the same.

Session 6 Tips:

1. Review the characteristics suggested by each Scripture passage. They are noted below:
   2 Timothy 3:16-17 – Scripture; knowing and living biblical truth
   Proverbs 27:17 – Accountability; being held accountable and holding others accountable
   Ephesians 4:11-13 – Spiritual Gifts; allowing the spiritual gifts of others to build you up, hold you up, and train you up
   James 1:2-4 – Life's Circumstances; processing these through the lens of faith rather than doubt; knowing God is growing you through your difficult circumstances
   1 Timothy 4:7b-8 – Spiritual Disciplines; being involved individually and as a community in spiritual disciplines
2. The spiritual disciplines your group suggest might include: Prayer, Bible study, Fasting, Worship, Silence, Evangelism, Sharing the Lord's Supper, Giving time, talents, or money, Serving others, Solitude, Meditation on or memorization of Scripture, etc.
3. When doing the commissioning experience, be certain you call each person by name. Pray that he or she will be available for God's use and that He would use each one.
4. Before the next meeting, tell the person who is inviting a non-Christian friend to fill the empty chair next week that you'll help in any way he or she would like.

ACKNOWLEDGMENTS:

Special thanks to the great leadership team that helped me to develop the initial concept for this study: Donna Rigdon, Rick Roepke, Brian Schutte, Christy Schutte, Scott Shoopman, Linda Trent, Terry Vogel, and Judy Vogel.

Other key contributors were Ben Colter and Ron Keck. Scott Lee provided art direction and interior design. The cover was designed by Clark Hook. The editorial team included Ben Colter, Sarah Hogg, and Lori Mayes.